Children's Atlas
of
Animals

Contents

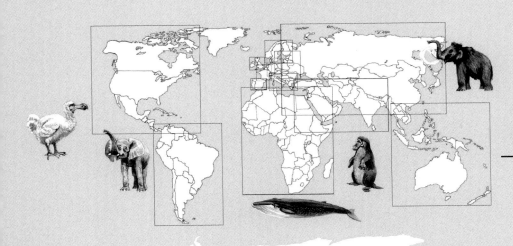

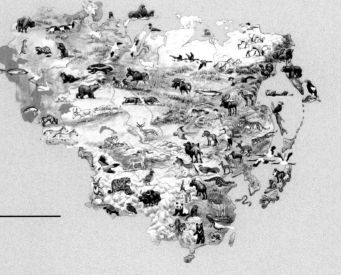

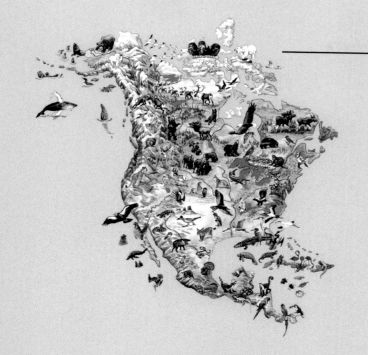
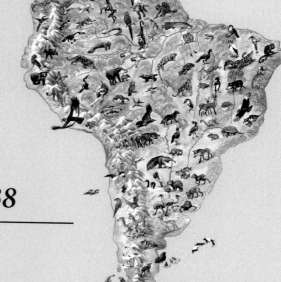

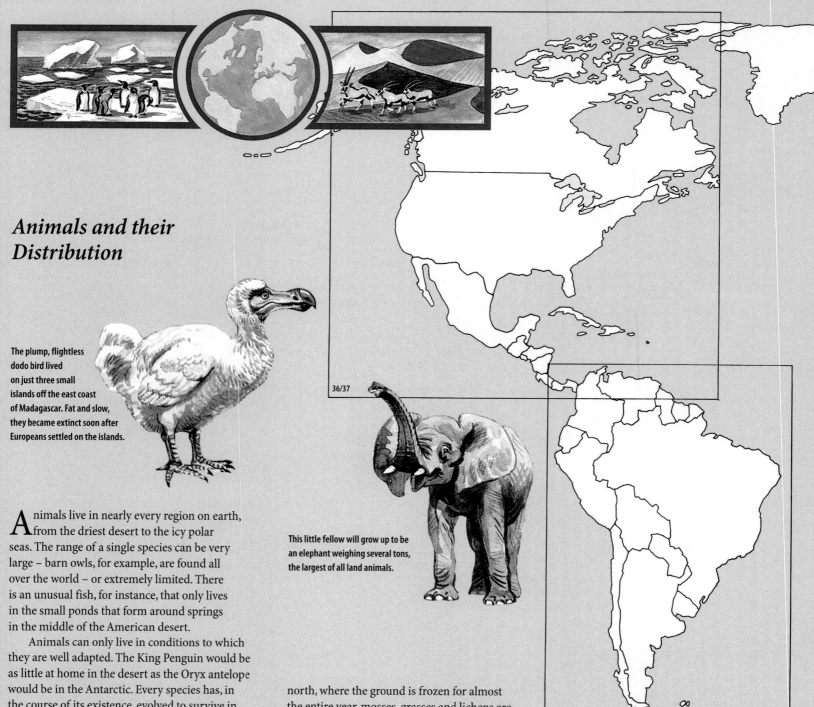

Animals and their Distribution

The plump, flightless dodo bird lived on just three small islands off the east coast of Madagascar. Fat and slow, they became extinct soon after Europeans settled on the islands.

This little fellow will grow up to be an elephant weighing several tons, the largest of all land animals.

36/37

38/39

Animals live in nearly every region on earth, from the driest desert to the icy polar seas. The range of a single species can be very large – barn owls, for example, are found all over the world – or extremely limited. There is an unusual fish, for instance, that only lives in the small ponds that form around springs in the middle of the American desert.

Animals can only live in conditions to which they are well adapted. The King Penguin would be as little at home in the desert as the Oryx antelope would be in the Antarctic. Every species has, in the course of its existence, evolved to survive in a very specific environment. Perhaps it has an especially thick fur coat, or the ability to live for an extended period of time without water. Animal habitats are defined by climate and the kind of plant life that grows there. Location also matters. Does the habitat lie on the equator, or in a snow-covered polar region? The landscape features, like mountains and lakes, also play a part, as does the distance from the sea. Forests only grow where the great trees can draw sufficient nutrients from a soil deep enough to accommodate their roots, preferably in a region where there is enough water all year round. Forest zones include the taiga, with its fir trees and birches, the temperate forest zone, where the trees are deciduous, mountain forests and, of course, the tropical rainforest. The steppes in northern Eurasia, prairies in North America and savannahs in the tropical south are examples of open grasslands, an environment where forests cannot gain a foothold. Far to the

north, where the ground is frozen for almost the entire year, mosses, grasses and lichens are characteristic of the Arctic tundra. Deserts are regions where very little rain falls and life is difficult for even the smallest plants and animals.

But it is not the environment alone that determines an animal's distribution on earth. Obstacles like seas, mountain ranges and deserts can stop a species from spreading further. As a result, each continent is home to

its own unique range of animals. Zoologists divide the earth geographically into six faunal zones: the High Arctic, Neo-tropical, Ethiopian, Oriental, Australasian and Oceanic.

Often, the present-day distribution of an animal species also provides information about the history of the earth itself. We know, for example, that 270 million years ago there was just one giant continent, Pangaea. Over time, and very slowly, perhaps just 4 in (10 cm) per year, the continents we know today drifted apart, to be separated by the great seas and oceans.

During the ice ages, the dropping sea level left land bridges between many of the continents for an extended period of time. North America and Asia, for example, were joined near Alaska.

THE GEOGRAPHIC FAUNAL ZONES OF THE EARTH

- High Arctic
- Neo-tropical
- Ethiopian
- Oriental
- Australasian
- Oceanic

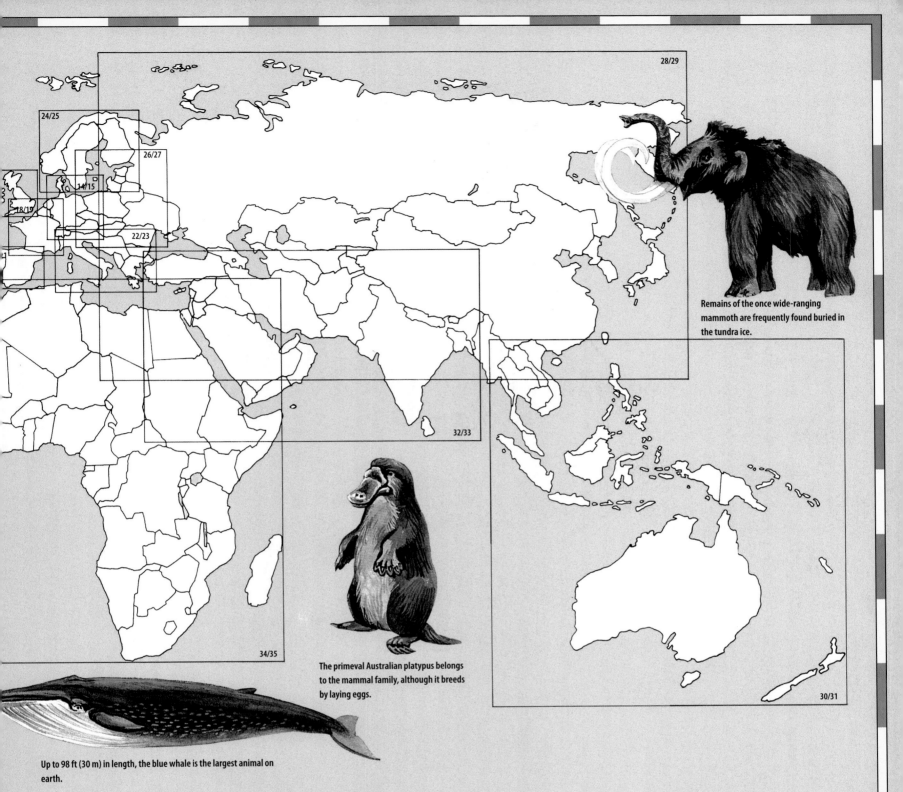

Remains of the once wide-ranging mammoth are frequently found buried in the tundra ice.

The primeval Australian platypus belongs to the mammal family, although it breeds by laying eggs.

Up to 98 ft (30 m) in length, the blue whale is the largest animal on earth.

The land bridge of Central America is still present today. The oddest animal worlds are the ones with many so-called "primeval" (early) species, like Australia. Their existence suggests a long period of isolation. In contrast, finding the same, or closely related, animal species on different continents indicates that there was once a physical connection between the land masses. Nevertheless, some animals manage to migrate to far distant lands despite geographical obstacles. Flying animals such as bats and birds have little difficulty crossing mountains and seas. Insects can travel long distances on the wind. Even land animals have succeeded in settling distant islands, travelling on floating tree trunks or rafts of vegetation. In this way lemurs came to Madagascar and the giant land tortoise made it to the Galapagos Islands. Finally, humans have also played a role in assisting the movement of animals between continents. Mice, rabbits and feral domestic animals can arrive in a different habitat via ship or airplane. People also tend to take along animals they find useful when they migrate. This is how the horse came from Europe to North America, and how forest animals suitable for hunting arrived in England from Asia.

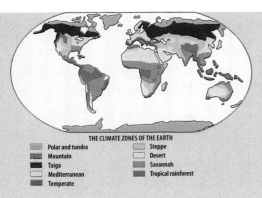

THE CLIMATE ZONES OF THE EARTH

Polar and tundra	Steppe
Mountain	Desert
Taiga	Savannah
Mediterranean	Tropical rainforest
Temperate	

270 million years ago, there was just one giant continent, called Pangaea.

Germany, Austria and Switzerland

Dense beech and oak forest once covered most of Germany, Switzerland and Austria. Today, a great many people live in this part of Europe, and the primeval forest has long been cleared. The trees growing today are non-native species grown for their timber. There is very little untouched, natural forest left. Small stretches can be found in the Bavarian Forest, Harz Mountains and Pfalz Forest. Happily, red deer, wildcats, wild pigs and the mufflon, a kind of sheep, are equally at home in a forest planted by humans as they are on their native mountain slopes. There are also many animals adapted to the drier steppe environment now living in the treeless landscape of field, meadow and hedgerow. The long-legged hare, as well as numerous species of butterfly and grasshopper, are among the species that enjoy farm life. The common buzzard, expanding its territory ever further westward, finds agricultural areas ideal for the hunt.

The great bustard, common in the eastern steppe regions, has recently been sighted in Germany. From a distance, this shy, heavy

The bearded vulture died out in the Alpine regions during the last century. Today, efforts are being made to reintroduce the species.

BALTIC SEA

NORTH SEA

200 km

100

0

① Mole
② Wild rabbit
③ Hare
④ Mountain (snow) hare
⑤ Alpine marmot
⑥ Beaver
⑦ Edible dormouse
⑧ White mouse
⑨ Fox
⑩ Tree martin
⑪ Mouse weasel
⑫ European otter
⑬ Wild cats
⑭ Seal
⑮ Wild pig
⑯ Red deer
⑰ Fallow deer
⑱ Roe deer
⑲ Ibex
⑳ Mufflon sheep
㉑ Chamois
㉒ Great crested grebe
㉓ Great white stork
㉔ Black stork
㉕ Sea eagle
㉖ Golden eagle
㉗ Goshawk
㉘ Common buzzard
㉙ Osprey
㉚ Peregrine falcon
㉛ Capercaillie (grouse)
㉜ Black grouse
㉝ Hazel grouse
㉞ Partridge
㉟ Great bustard
㊱ Crane
㊲ Oyster catcher
㊳ Lapwing
㊴ Ringed plover
㊵ Black-tailed godwit
㊶ Sandpiper
㊷ Redshank
㊸ Dunlin
㊹ Common snipe
㊺ Ibis
㊻ Little owl
㊼ Eagle owl
㊽ Alpine swift

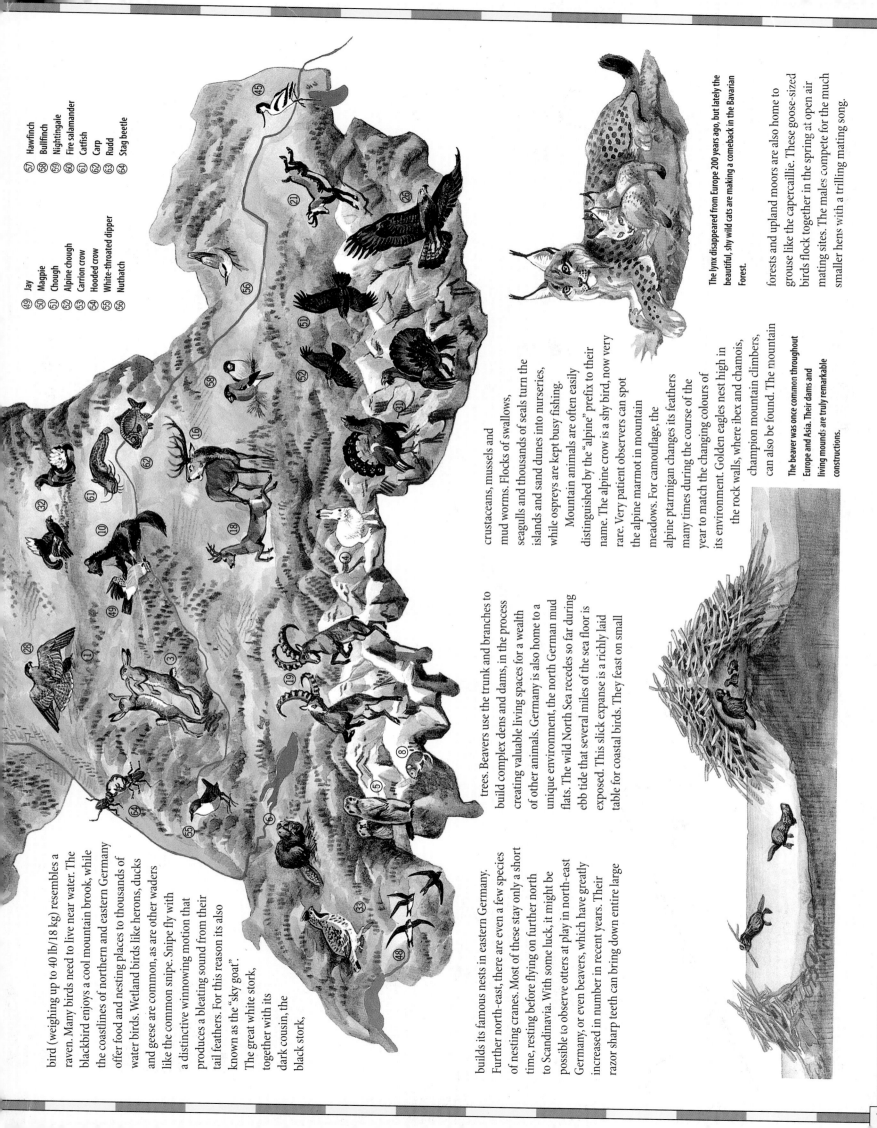

49 Jay
50 Magpie
51 Chough
52 Alpine chough
53 Carrion crow
54 Hooded crow
55 White-throated dipper
56 Nuthatch

57 Hawfinch
58 Bullfinch
59 Nightingale
60 Fire salamander
61 Catfish
62 Carp
63 Rudd
64 Stag beetle

bird (weighing up to 40 lb/18 kg) resembles a raven. Many birds need to live near water. The blackbird enjoys a cool mountain brook, while the coastlines of northern and eastern Germany offer food and nesting places to thousands of water birds. Wetland birds like herons, ducks and geese are common, as are other waders like the common snipe. Snipe fly with a distinctive winnowing motion that produces a bleating sound from their tail feathers. For this reason its also known as the "sky goat". The great white stork, together with its dark cousin, the black stork,

builds its famous nests in eastern Germany. Further north-east, there are even a few species of nesting cranes. Most of these stay only a short time, resting before flying on further north to Scandinavia. With some luck, it might be possible to observe otters at play in north-east Germany, or even beavers, which have greatly increased in number in recent years. Their razor sharp teeth can bring down entire large

trees. Beavers use the trunk and branches to build complex dens and dams, in the process creating valuable living spaces for a wealth of other animals. Germany is also home to a unique environment, the north German mud flats. The wild North Sea recedes so far during ebb tide that several miles of the sea floor is exposed. This slick expanse is a richly laid table for coastal birds. They feast on small

crustaceans, mussels and mud worms. Flocks of swallows, seagulls and thousands of seals turn the islands and sand dunes into nurseries, while ospreys are kept busy fishing.

Mountain animals are often easily distinguished by the "alpine" prefix to their name. The alpine crow is a shy bird, now very rare. Very patient observers can spot the alpine marmot in mountain meadows. For camouflage, the alpine ptarmigan changes its feathers many times during the course of the year to match the changing colours of its environment. Golden eagles nest high in the rock walls, where ibex and chamois, champion mountain climbers, can also be found. The mountain

The lynx disappeared from Europe 200 years ago, but lately the beautiful, shy wild cats are making a comeback in the Bavarian Forest.

forests and upland moors are also home to grouse like the capercaillie. These goose-sized birds flock together in the spring at open air mating sites. The males compete for the much smaller hens with a trilling mating song.

The beaver was once common throughout Europe and Asia. Their dams and living mounds are truly remarkable constructions.

ATLANTIC OCEAN

Great Britain and Ireland

The British Isles are located in the northern Atlantic not far from the north-west coast of France. During the ice ages, the large island of Great Britain, where England, Scotland and Wales are found, was part of the European mainland.

It was only with the melting of the glaciers some 9,000 years ago that sea levels rose and what is today the English Channel filled with water. The smaller island of Ireland has been an island for a longer period of time, since approximately 11,000 years ago. Before the islands became separated from the mainland, animals and plants common in the rest of Europe migrated into these northern areas. For this reason, many species found in the British Isles today are also native to central Europe. In geological terms, the period of time since the last ice age has been short, too short to permit the development of a uniquely evolved, starkly different world of animals.

The proximity of the sea gives the British Isles a characteristically oceanic climate. This means winters are mild, but very rainy, and summers are relatively cool. The rough Scottish highlands have a climate that resembles that of the Siberian tundra. Low mosses, lichens, low grasses and scrub define the landscape. Wet, cold storm winds blow over the rocky moors even in midsummer. A few animals

200 km

100

0

1. Mole
2. Hedgehog
3. Wild rabbit
4. Hare
5. Mountain (snow) hare
6. Red squirrel
7. Grey squirrel
8. Fox
9. Badger
10. Mink
11. Otter
12. Wild cat
13. Seal
14. Right whale
15. Shetland pony
16. Red deer
17. Fallow deer
18. Sika deer
19. Roe deer
20. Muntjac
21. Wool sheep
22. Wild cattle
23. Highland cattle
24. Wallaby
25. Dwarf grebe
26. Shearwater
27. Puffin
28. Northern gannet
29. Crow
30. Cormorant
31. Grey heron

ENGLISH CHANNEL

found here are adapted to a tundra climate, like the snow hare or snowy owl, the latter a rare winter visitor from the far north. Animals that require a warmer, drier summer prefer the mild climate of southern England. Even the wallaby, accidentally introduced into the wild from Australia, can survive here.

Almost all the forests in the British Isles have been cleared at one time or another. The great seagoing empire needed the wood to build its ships. As a result, nearly every large forest animal – including bear, wolf, lynx and wild pig – has been gone for a long time. Deep green meadows, wild hedgerows and hilly moorlands are the distinguishing features of England, Ireland and Wales today. There are plump sheep grazing everywhere. Small forest animals like foxes, blackbirds and robins make their homes in idyllic estate parks and gardens with ancient, towering trees. The diverse species of bird living in the British Isles is world famous, including its many kinds of

native sea bird, among them the sea swallow, a variety of common tern, that flies like an arrow through the waves. The cormorant swims so deep in the water that only its head and neck are above the surface. The puffin, though actually a skilful flier and swimmer, often lands in an ungraceful belly flop. Like the guillemot, puffins nest in enormous colonies on steep cliff faces along the coast and nearby islets, where they are safe from predators. Mighty fin, humpback and right whales swim by off the coast of the small rocky islands of northern Scotland.

The British have always been passionate breeders of domestic animal species. The mighty Shire horse looks like a giant next to the tiny Shetland pony.

The musk deer, sika deer and muntjac were introduced into England from Asia.

32 Mute swan
33 Pochard duck
34 Ring-necked duck
35 Common shelduck
36 Eider duck
37 Merganser
38 Peregrine falcon
39 Merlin
40 Scottish moorhen
41 Capercaillie (grouse)
42 Black grouse
43 Pheasant
44 Moorhen
45 Osprey
46 Woodcock
47 Curlew
48 Black-backed gull
49 Long-eared owl
50 Snowy owl
51 Barn owl
52 Kingfisher
53 Green woodpecker
54 Blackbird
55 Alpine crow
56 Raven
57 Robin
58 Monkfish
59 Torpedo fish
60 Salmon
61 Whiting
62 Atlantic cod
63 Eel
64 Sea bream
65 Catfish
66 Turbot
67 Squid
68 Mussel

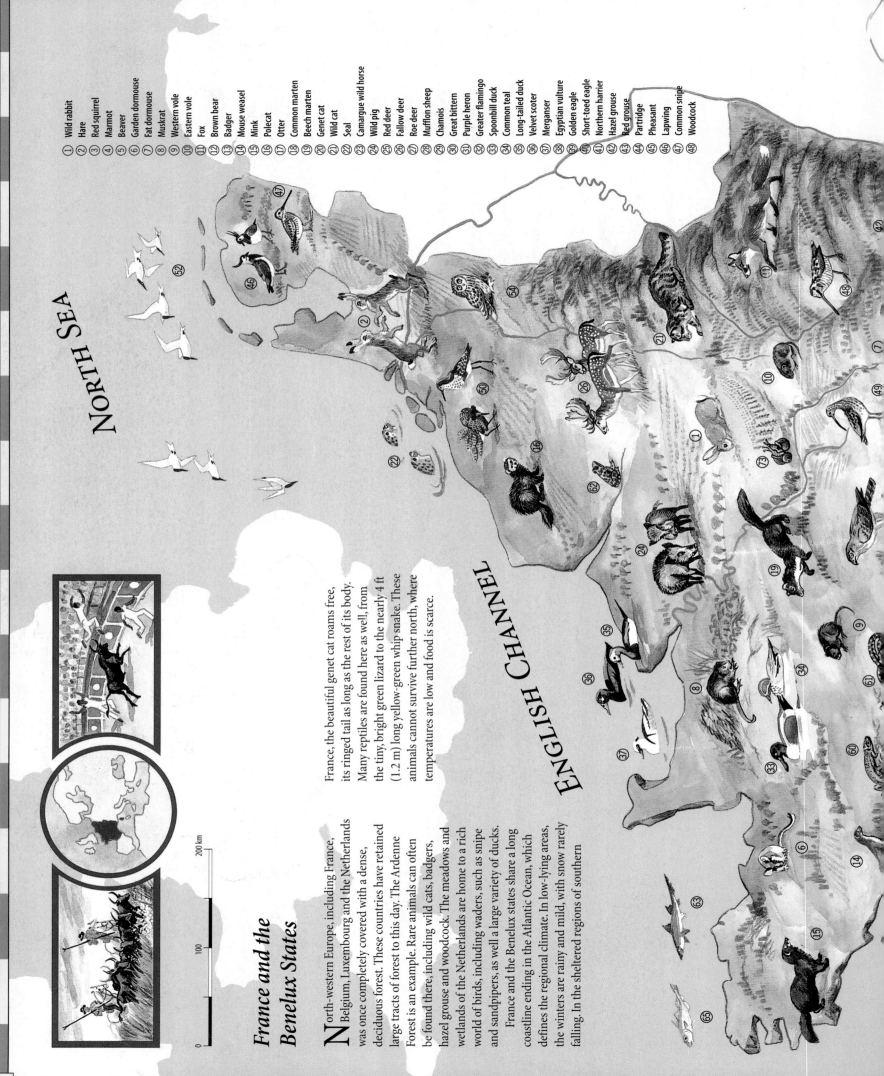

NORTH SEA

ENGLISH CHANNEL

France and the Benelux States

North-western Europe, including France, Belgium, Luxembourg and the Netherlands was once completely covered with a dense, deciduous forest. These countries have retained large tracts of forest to this day. The Ardenne Forest is an example. Rare animals can often be found there, including wild cats, badgers, hazel grouse and woodcock. The meadows and wetlands of the Netherlands are home to a rich world of birds, including waders, such as snipe and sandpipers, as well as a large variety of ducks.

France and the Benelux states share a long coastline ending in the Atlantic Ocean, which defines the regional climate. In low-lying areas, the winters are rainy and mild, with snow rarely falling. In the sheltered regions of southern France, the beautiful genet cat roams free, its ringed tail as long as the rest of its body. Many reptiles are found here as well, from the tiny, bright green lizard to the nearly 4 ft (1.2 m) long yellow-green whip snake. These animals cannot survive further north, where temperatures are low and food is scarce.

1. Wild rabbit
2. Hare
3. Red squirrel
4. Marmot
5. Beaver
6. Garden dormouse
7. Fat dormouse
8. Muskrat
9. Western vole
10. Eastern vole
11. Fox
12. Brown bear
13. Badger
14. Mouse weasel
15. Mink
16. Polecat
17. Otter
18. Common marten
19. Beech marten
20. Genet cat
21. Wild cat
22. Seal
23. Camargue wild horse
24. Wild pig
25. Red deer
26. Fallow deer
27. Roe deer
28. Mufflon sheep
29. Chamois
30. Great bittern
31. Purple heron
32. Greater flamingo
33. Spoonbill duck
34. Common teal
35. Long-tailed duck
36. Velvet scoter
37. Merganser
38. Egyptian vulture
39. Golden eagle
40. Short-toed eagle
41. Northern harrier
42. Hazel grouse
43. Red grouse
44. Partridge
45. Pheasant
46. Lapwing
47. Common snipe
48. Woodcock

200 km

100

0

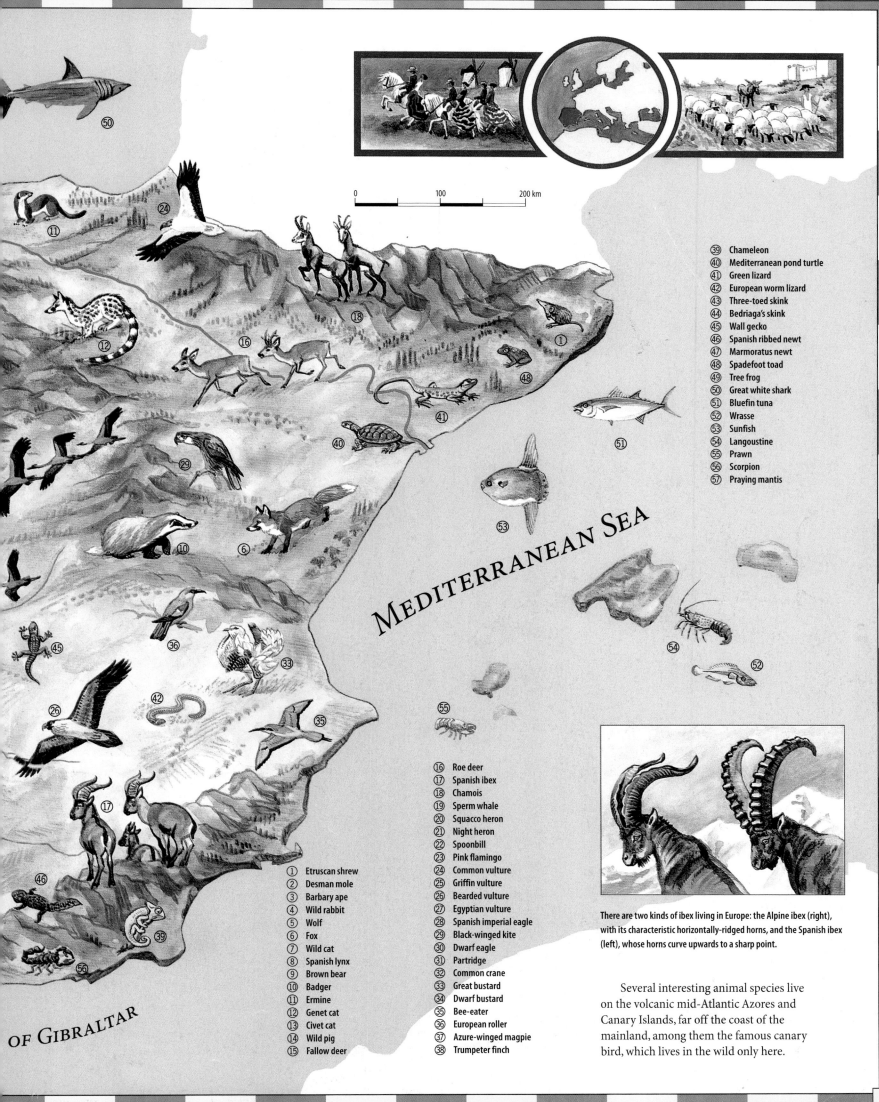

MEDITERRANEAN SEA

OF GIBRALTAR

39 Chameleon
40 Mediterranean pond turtle
41 Green lizard
42 European worm lizard
43 Three-toed skink
44 Bedriaga's skink
45 Wall gecko
46 Spanish ribbed newt
47 Marmoratus newt
48 Spadefoot toad
49 Tree frog
50 Great white shark
51 Bluefin tuna
52 Wrasse
53 Sunfish
54 Langoustine
55 Prawn
56 Scorpion
57 Praying mantis

1 Etruscan shrew
2 Desman mole
3 Barbary ape
4 Wild rabbit
5 Wolf
6 Fox
7 Wild cat
8 Spanish lynx
9 Brown bear
10 Badger
11 Ermine
12 Genet cat
13 Civet cat
14 Wild pig
15 Fallow deer

16 Roe deer
17 Spanish ibex
18 Chamois
19 Sperm whale
20 Squacco heron
21 Night heron
22 Spoonbill
23 Pink flamingo
24 Common vulture
25 Griffin vulture
26 Bearded vulture
27 Egyptian vulture
28 Spanish imperial eagle
29 Black-winged kite
30 Dwarf eagle
31 Partridge
32 Common crane
33 Great bustard
34 Dwarf bustard
35 Bee-eater
36 European roller
37 Azure-winged magpie
38 Trumpeter finch

There are two kinds of ibex living in Europe: the Alpine ibex (right), with its characteristic horizontally-ridged horns, and the Spanish ibex (left), whose horns curve upwards to a sharp point.

Several interesting animal species live on the volcanic mid-Atlantic Azores and Canary Islands, far off the coast of the mainland, among them the famous canary bird, which lives in the wild only here.

According to legend, Romulus and Remus, the twin founders of Rome, were nursed by a she-wolf.

Italy, Greece and the Slavic States

Summers are hot and dry in the countries of the eastern Mediterranean. Winters are mild and wet. The forests that once grew here have been nearly completely cleared, mostly for shipbuilding, with a few small exceptions. Today, the landscape is dominated by olive groves, vineyards and dry shrub lands known as maquis.

This wide-open habitat is home to numerous songbirds, like the sylvia and mockingbird, which benefit from its rich insect life and sheltered nesting places. The hot summer nights are filled with the never-ending trill of the cicadas,

In Italy, the primeval-looking domestic water buffalo is a common sight. Its wild forebears came from India.

as tortoises and lizards rest on stones warmed by the Mediterranean sun. Wall geckos are frequent visitors, their gripping toes running up and down the smoothest house and garden walls with ease. Chameleons, an introduced species from Africa, are also common.

MEDITERRANEAN SEA

ADRIATIC SEA

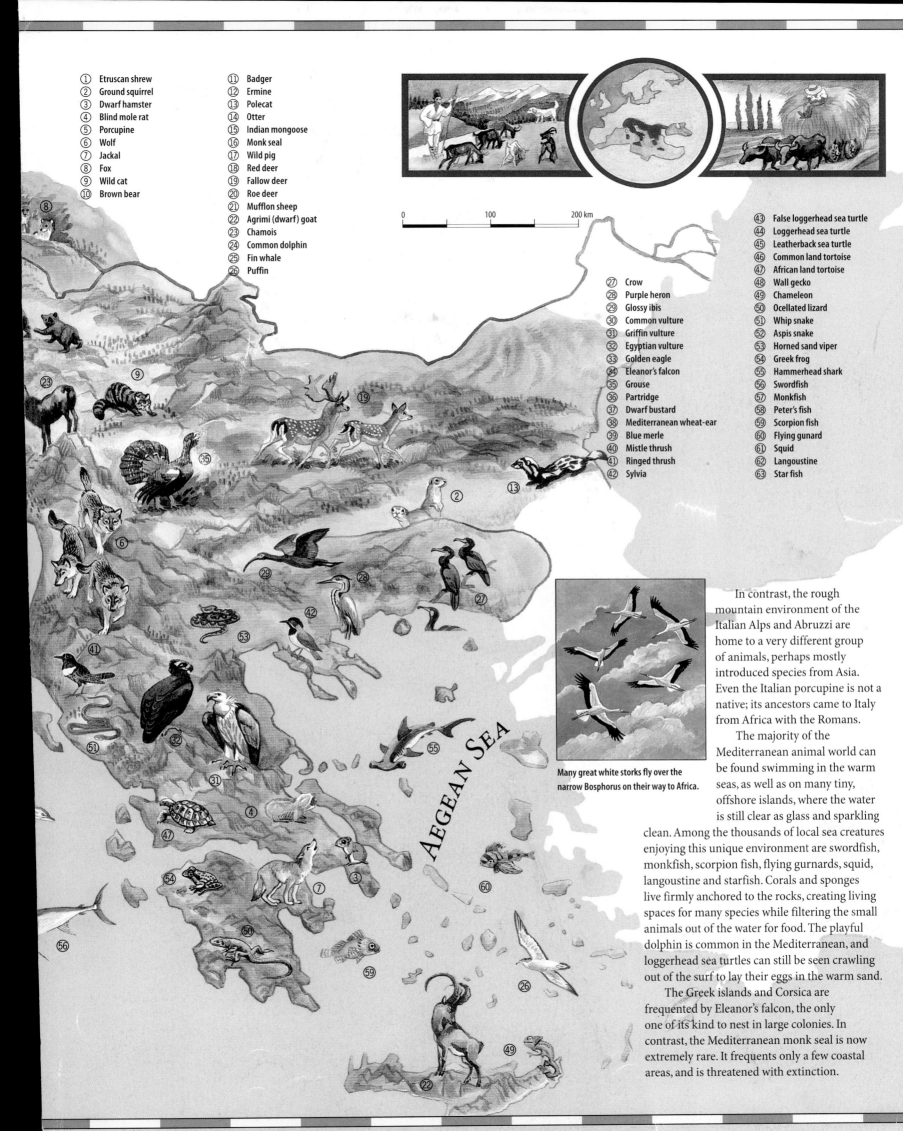

1. Etruscan shrew
2. Ground squirrel
3. Dwarf hamster
4. Blind mole rat
5. Porcupine
6. Wolf
7. Jackal
8. Fox
9. Wild cat
10. Brown bear
11. Badger
12. Ermine
13. Polecat
14. Otter
15. Indian mongoose
16. Monk seal
17. Wild pig
18. Red deer
19. Fallow deer
20. Roe deer
21. Mufflon sheep
22. Agrimi (dwarf) goat
23. Chamois
24. Common dolphin
25. Fin whale
26. Puffin

27. Crow
28. Purple heron
29. Glossy ibis
30. Common vulture
31. Griffin vulture
32. Egyptian vulture
33. Golden eagle
34. Eleanor's falcon
35. Grouse
36. Partridge
37. Dwarf bustard
38. Mediterranean wheat-ear
39. Blue merle
40. Mistle thrush
41. Ringed thrush
42. Sylvia

43. False loggerhead sea turtle
44. Loggerhead sea turtle
45. Leatherback sea turtle
46. Common land tortoise
47. African land tortoise
48. Wall gecko
49. Chameleon
50. Ocellated lizard
51. Whip snake
52. Aspis snake
53. Horned sand viper
54. Greek frog
55. Hammerhead shark
56. Swordfish
57. Monkfish
58. Peter's fish
59. Scorpion fish
60. Flying gunard
61. Squid
62. Langoustine
63. Star fish

0   100   200 km

AEGEAN SEA

Many great white storks fly over the narrow Bosphorus on their way to Africa.

In contrast, the rough mountain environment of the Italian Alps and Abruzzi are home to a very different group of animals, perhaps mostly introduced species from Asia. Even the Italian porcupine is not a native; its ancestors came to Italy from Africa with the Romans.

The majority of the Mediterranean animal world can be found swimming in the warm seas, as well as on many tiny, offshore islands, where the water is still clear as glass and sparkling clean. Among the thousands of local sea creatures enjoying this unique environment are swordfish, monkfish, scorpion fish, flying gurnards, squid, langoustine and starfish. Corals and sponges live firmly anchored to the rocks, creating living spaces for many species while filtering the small animals out of the water for food. The playful dolphin is common in the Mediterranean, and loggerhead sea turtles can still be seen crawling out of the surf to lay their eggs in the warm sand.

The Greek islands and Corsica are frequented by Eleanor's falcon, the only one of its kind to nest in large colonies. In contrast, the Mediterranean monk seal is now extremely rare. It frequents only a few coastal areas, and is threatened with extinction.

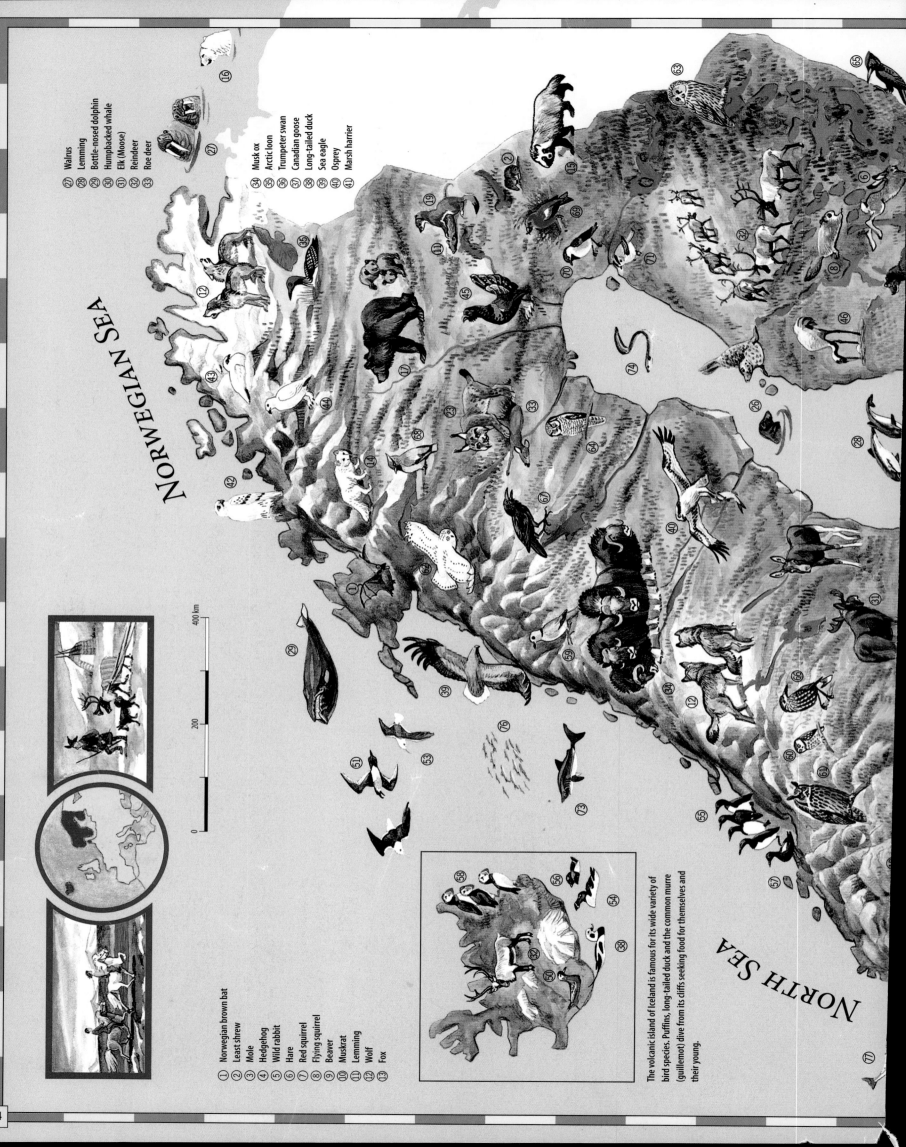

NORWEGIAN SEA

NORTH SEA

① Norwegian brown bat
② Least shrew
③ Mole
④ Hedgehog
⑤ Wild rabbit
⑥ Hare
⑦ Red squirrel
⑧ Flying squirrel
⑨ Beaver
⑩ Muskrat
⑪ Lemming
⑫ Wolf
⑬ Fox

㉗ Walrus
㉘ Lemming
㉙ Bottle-nosed dolphin
㉚ Humpbacked whale
㉛ Elk (Moose)
㉜ Reindeer
㉝ Roe deer

㉞ Musk ox
㉟ Arctic loon
㊱ Trumpeter swan
㊲ Canadian goose
㊳ Long-tailed duck
㊴ Sea eagle
㊵ Osprey
㊶ Marsh harrier

400 km

200

0

The volcanic island of Iceland is famous for its wide variety of bird species. Puffins, long-tailed duck and the common murre (guillemot) dive from its cliffs seeking food for themselves and their young.

Scandinavia

Scandinavia lies in the icy far north of Europe, so far north that parts of it lie within the Arctic Circle. The fish-rich coastal regions of Norway are home to a typically arctic range of animals, including the walrus, polar bear and several species of seal. Further south, extensive deciduous and mixed pine forests, rugged mountain ranges and large lake districts offer a range of exceptionally diverse habitats, including forested taiga and bare, grassy tundra.

The lynx, wolf and wolverine wander through the forests searching for prey. The powerful, fearless wolverine is known as the "glutton" in the native Scandinavian languages, a name it carries not because it eats more than other animals, but because the word for glutton in Norwegian sounds like the word "fjellfoss", which means "mountain cat". It is even still possible to meet a brown bear in the wild here. Every year, thousands of salmon swim upstream returning to the rivers of their birth to lay their own eggs. They leap some 10 ft (3 m) in the air against the current, covering a distance of 20 ft (6 m) with one jump. After laying their eggs, they return to the sea. Life is hard during the cold, long northern winter. In the spring, cranes and wading birds like the sandpiper, as well as many other species of bird, return to Scandinavia from their winter migration to the warm south, flying across the European mainland to Africa and the Mediterranean regions. The larger inhabitants of the taiga and tundra are better adapted to the difficult climate. The mighty elk strides through the snow on its long legs, while the patient reindeer searches beneath the snow for lichens and roots. Great herds of reindeer cross into the tundra regions during the summer; for the winter, the forested taiga provides more nutrition and protection.

The Laplanders, members of the Sami indigenous group living in the north of Norway, Sweden and Finland, domesticated the reindeer many centuries ago. Even today, the Sami nomadically follow the herds back and forth. Reindeer provide them with meat, milk, leather and fur, as well as being strong work and transportation animals. Sixty years ago, the primeval-looking musk ox was reintroduced in Scandinavia. Long extinct on the continent, they once roamed across the whole of Europe.

14	Arctic fox	42	Gyrfalcon
15	Marten	43	Ptarmigan
16	Polar bear	44	Moorhen
17	Brown bear	45	Grouse
18	Wolverine	46	Crane
19	Ermine	47	Oystercatcher
20	Marten	48	Golden plover
21	Sable	49	Sandpiper
22	Otter	50	Northern (red-necked) phalarope
23	Lynx	51	Arctic skua
24	Sea lion	52	Caspian tern
25	Ringed seal	53	Herring gull
26	Grey seal	54	Lesser auk
		55	Guillemot (common murre)
60	Pygmy owl	56	Dovekie
61	Eagle owl	57	Black Guillemot
62	Snowy owl	58	Puffin
63	Ural owl	59	Eurasian collared dove
64	Northern hawk owl		
65	Black woodpecker		
66	Nutcracker		
67	Raven		
68	Waxwing		
69	Common crossbill		
70	Siberian tit		
71	Goldcrest		
72	Sea lamprey		
73	Porbeagle (shark)		
74	Common eel		
75	Conger eel		
76	Herring		
77	Salmon		

BALTIC SEA

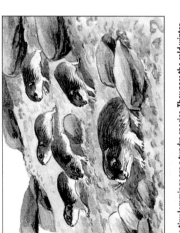

The plumage of the ptarmigan changes twice a year, the number of times that the seasons change in the tundra. It is as well camouflaged in its snow-white winter feathers as it is in the summer, when its plumage is a variegated brown. Many predators, like the arctic fox and ermine, find them nevertheless.

The tiny lemmings are a tundra species. They pass the cold winter months in well-designed tunnels dug deep under the thick snow.

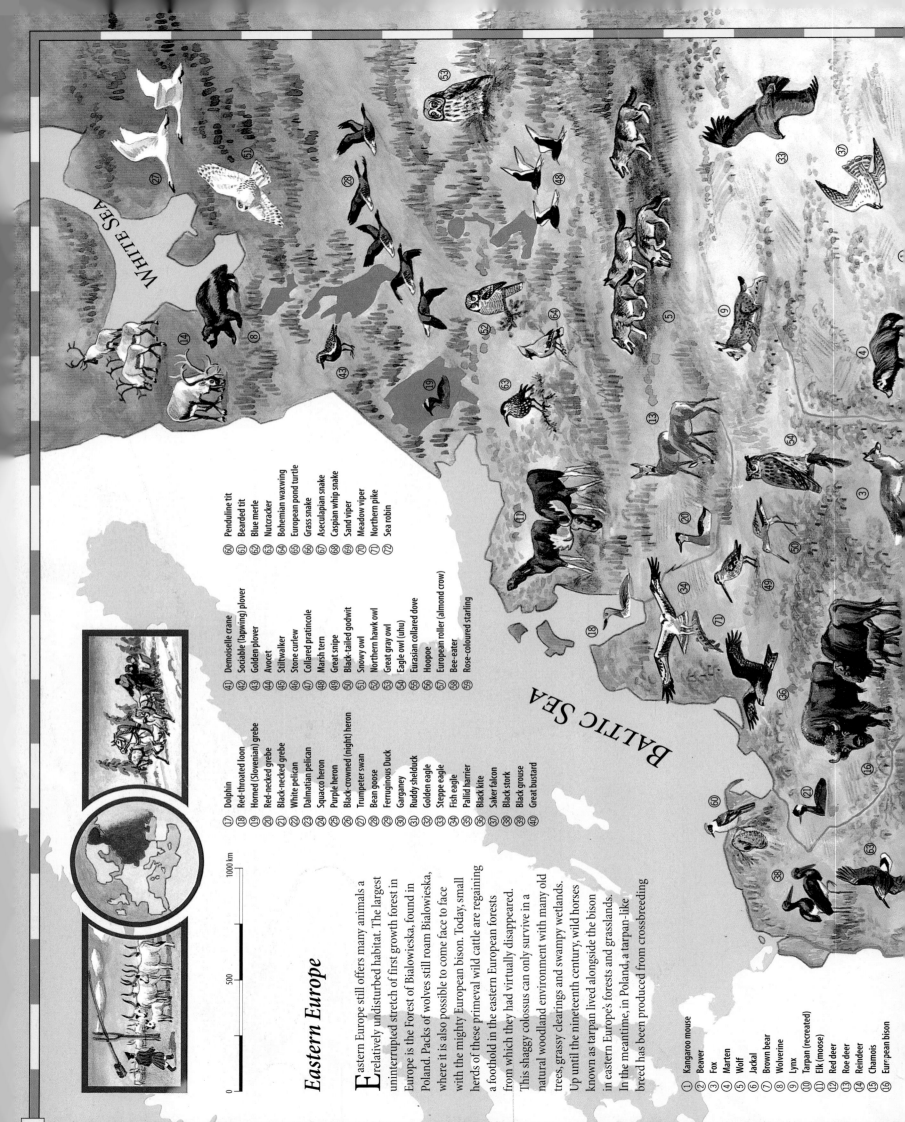

Eastern Europe

Eastern Europe still offers many animals a relatively undisturbed habitat. The largest uninterrupted stretch of first growth forest in Europe is the Forest of Bialowieska, found in Poland. Packs of wolves still roam Bialowieska, where it is also possible to come face to face with the mighty European bison. Today, small herds of these primeval wild cattle are regaining a foothold in the eastern European forests from which they had virtually disappeared. This shaggy colossus can only survive in a natural woodland environment with many old trees, grassy clearings and swampy wetlands. Up until the nineteenth century, wild horses known as tarpan lived alongside the bison in eastern Europe's forests and grasslands. In the meantime, in Poland, a tarpan-like breed has been produced from crossbreeding

WHITE SEA

BALTIC SEA

0   500   1000 km

1 Kangaroo mouse
2 Beaver
3 Fox
4 Marten
5 Wolf
6 Jackal
7 Brown bear
8 Wolverine
9 Lynx
10 Tarpan (recreated)
11 Elk (moose)
12 Red deer
13 Roe deer
14 Reindeer
15 Chamois
16 European bison

17 Dolphin
18 Red-throated loon
19 Horned (Slovenian) grebe
20 Red-necked grebe
21 Black-necked grebe
22 White pelican
23 Dalmatian pelican
24 Squacco heron
25 Purple heron
26 Black-crowned (night) heron
27 Trumpeter swan
28 Bean goose
29 Ferruginous Duck
30 Garganey
31 Ruddy shelduck
32 Golden eagle
33 Steppe eagle
34 Fish eagle
35 Pallid harrier
36 Black kite
37 Saker falcon
38 Black stork
39 Black grouse
40 Great bustard

41 Demoiselle crane
42 Sociable (lapwing) plover
43 Golden plover
44 Avocet
45 Stiltwalker
46 Stone curlew
47 Collared pratincole
48 Marsh tern
49 Great snipe
50 Black-tailed godwit
51 Snowy owl
52 Northern hawk owl
53 Great gray owl
54 Eagle owl (uhu)
55 Eurasian collared dove
56 Hoopoe
57 European roller (almond crow)
58 Bee-eater
59 Rose-coloured starling

60 Penduline tit
61 Bearded tit
62 Blue merle
63 Nutcracker
64 Bohemian waxwing
65 European pond turtle
66 Grass snake
67 Aesculapian snake
68 Caspian whip snake
69 Sand viper
70 Meadow viper
71 Northern pike
72 Sea robin

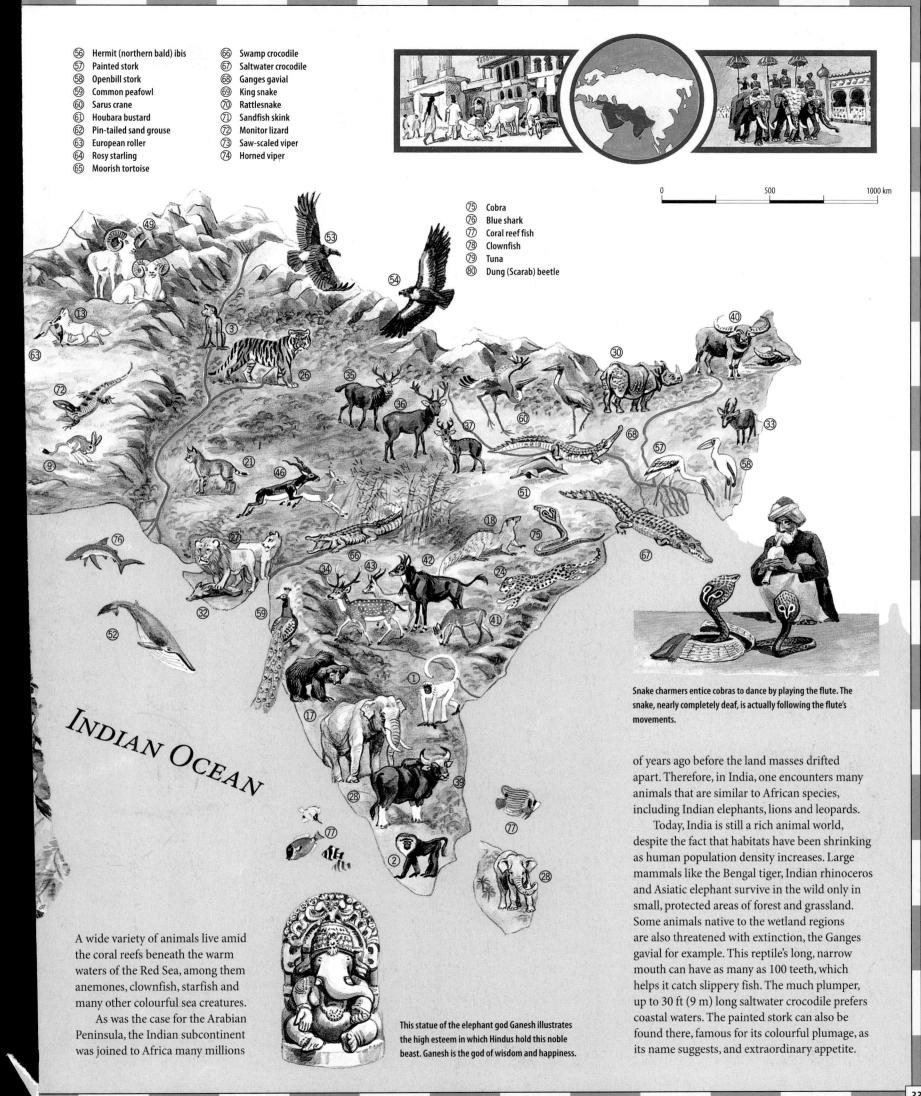

56 Hermit (northern bald) ibis
57 Painted stork
58 Openbill stork
59 Common peafowl
60 Sarus crane
61 Houbara bustard
62 Pin-tailed sand grouse
63 European roller
64 Rosy starling
65 Moorish tortoise

66 Swamp crocodile
67 Saltwater crocodile
68 Ganges gavial
69 King snake
70 Rattlesnake
71 Sandfish skink
72 Monitor lizard
73 Saw-scaled viper
74 Horned viper

75 Cobra
76 Blue shark
77 Coral reef fish
78 Clownfish
79 Tuna
80 Dung (Scarab) beetle

0   500   1000 km

INDIAN OCEAN

Snake charmers entice cobras to dance by playing the flute. The snake, nearly completely deaf, is actually following the flute's movements.

This statue of the elephant god Ganesh illustrates the high esteem in which Hindus hold this noble beast. Ganesh is the god of wisdom and happiness.

A wide variety of animals live amid the coral reefs beneath the warm waters of the Red Sea, among them anemones, clownfish, starfish and many other colourful sea creatures.

As was the case for the Arabian Peninsula, the Indian subcontinent was joined to Africa many millions of years ago before the land masses drifted apart. Therefore, in India, one encounters many animals that are similar to African species, including Indian elephants, lions and leopards.

Today, India is still a rich animal world, despite the fact that habitats have been shrinking as human population density increases. Large mammals like the Bengal tiger, Indian rhinoceros and Asiatic elephant survive in the wild only in small, protected areas of forest and grassland. Some animals native to the wetland regions are also threatened with extinction, the Ganges gavial for example. This reptile's long, narrow mouth can have as many as 100 teeth, which helps it catch slippery fish. The much plumper, up to 30 ft (9 m) long saltwater crocodile prefers coastal waters. The painted stork can also be found there, famous for its colourful plumage, as its name suggests, and extraordinary appetite.

Africa

Desert, savannah and rainforest are Africa's three most important environmental zones. The unbearably hot sun burns all day in the Sahara region, the largest continuous desert on earth. Rocky outcrops, the thin vegetation of the bordering Sahel, and barren sand dunes define the harsh landscape. The survival artists of the African desert include the Sahara gazelle, the small ungulate hyrax and the desert fox, also known as the fennec fox. The latter extends its enormous ears so as to catch the dry desert wind, reducing its body temperature. Better living conditions can be found in

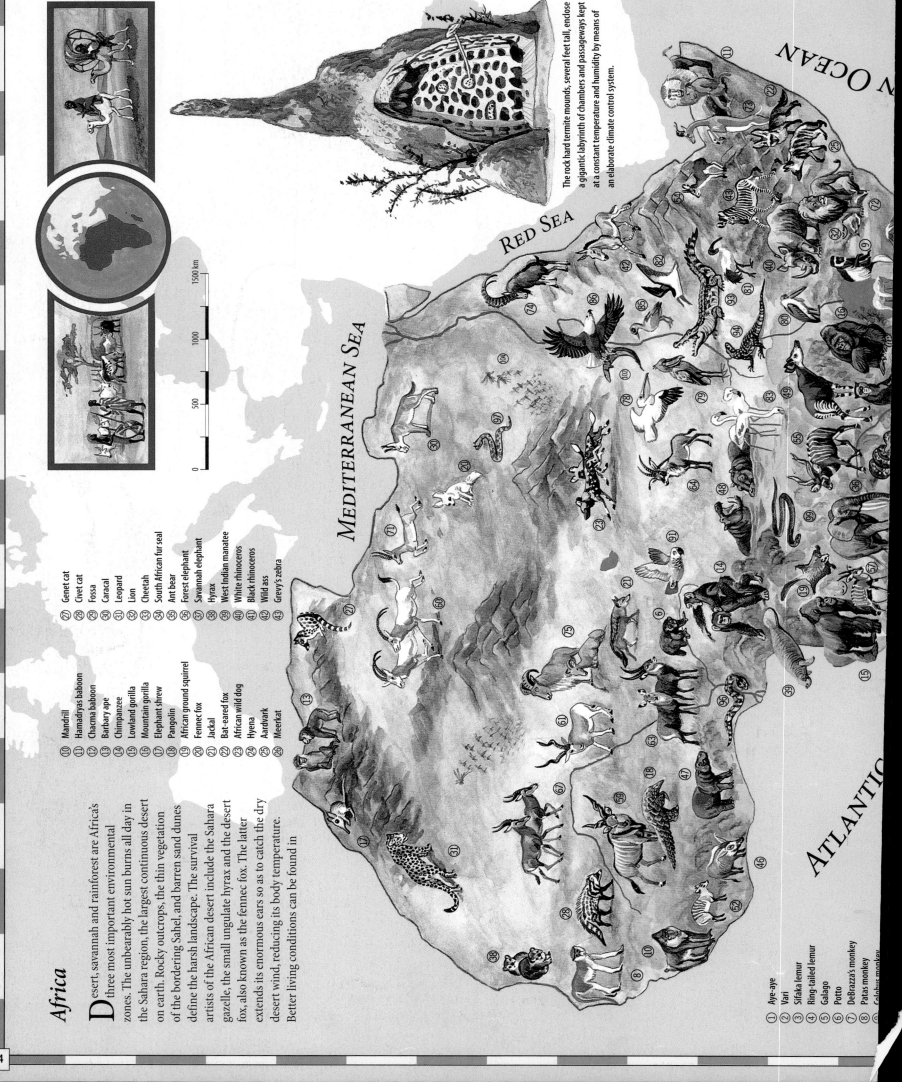

The rock hard termite mounds, several feet tall, enclose a gigantic labyrinth of chambers and passageways kept at a constant temperature and humidity by means of an elaborate climate control system.

1500 km
1000
500
0

MEDITERRANEAN SEA

RED SEA

ATLANTIC

N OCEAN

1 Aye-aye
2 Vari
3 Sifaka lemur
4 Ring-tailed lemur
5 Galago
6 Potto
7 DeBrazza's monkey
8 Patas monkey

10 Mandrill
11 Hamadryas baboon
12 Chacma baboon
13 Barbary ape
14 Chimpanzee
15 Lowland gorilla
16 Mountain gorilla
17 Elephant shrew
18 Pangolin
19 African ground squirrel
20 Fennec fox
21 Jackal
22 Bat-eared fox
23 African wild dog
24 Hyena
25 Aardvark
26 Meerkat

27 Genet cat
28 Civet cat
29 Fossa
30 Caracal
31 Leopard
32 Lion
33 Cheetah
34 South African fur seal
35 Ant bear
36 Forest elephant
37 Savannah elephant
38 Hyrax
39 West Indian manatee
40 White rhinoceros
41 Black rhinoceros
42 Wild ass
43 Grevy's zebra

The small fennec fox, also known as the desert fox, hunts throughout the cold desert night, putting its thick fur coat to good use.

smaller animals on the savannah, such as the long-legged secretary bird and social meerkats, the latter standing straight up in front of its den scanning the horizon for danger. The island of Madagascar has a particularly unique range of animal species, a result of its having drifted away from the African mainland some 280 million years ago. At some point in time, lemurs from the mainland made their way to the island. In other parts of the world these ancient prosimians have barely managed to survive, but

on Madagascar, isolated from large predators, they have flourished. The coelacanth, an ancient fish long thought to be extinct, was found in deep waters off the African coast. The nearest relatives of this four-finned fish left the sea for land many millions of years ago, the forefathers of all amphibians, reptiles, birds and mammals.

the wetlands like the Nile River valley and the southern Sudan. Crocodiles, hippopotami and water birds like the rare shoebill and African fish eagle are found. South of the Sahara, the rainforest belt runs east-west straight across central Africa. The smaller forest elephant, pygmy hippopotamus and shy Okapi, a short-necked forest giraffe, make these forests their home. Chimpanzees and gorillas, our nearest relatives in the animal kingdom, also favour the rainforest. The most famous African habitat is the savannah. The savannah consists of virtually uninterrupted, flat grassland scattered with acacia trees, interspersed with waterholes and swampy wetlands. Here as well, the daylight hours are brutally hot. Many parts of the savannah have a long dry season during which nearly all plant life shrivels from lack of moisture.

Yet there is nowhere else on earth with so great a variety of large mammals. Enormous herds of zebra, gnu, Cape buffalo, antelope and gazelle wander across the wide plains searching for grazing land and water, trailed by a host of predators, including lions, hyenas, leopards and cheetah. Vultures circle in the air above, waiting for the kill. Only the largest land animal of all, the giant African savannah elephant, has little to fear from the predators. There are also

One of the most dangerous animals in Africa is the tiny tse-tse fly. One bite can bring on the dreaded sleeping sickness, a devastating illness that can kill.

Africa is home to more varieties of antelope than anywhere else in the world. Each species can be identified by its horns.

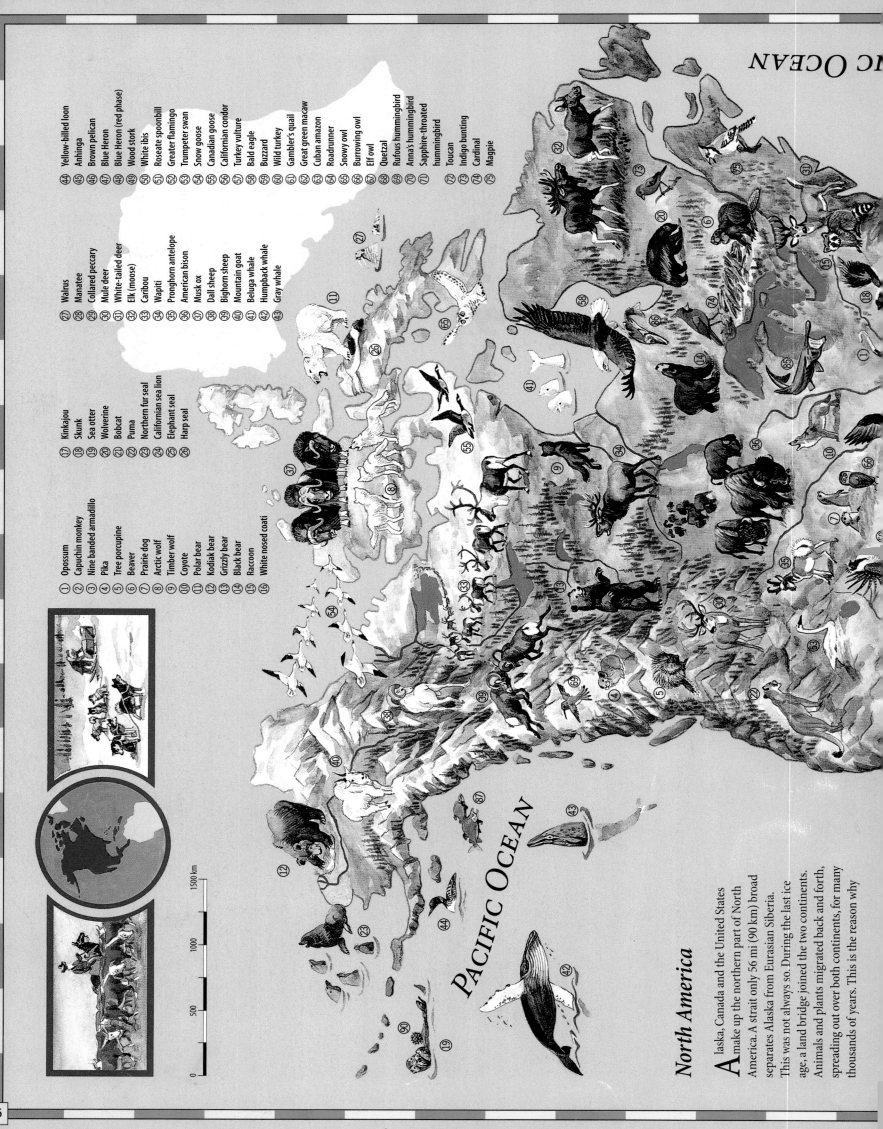

North America

Alaska, Canada and the United States make up the northern part of North America. A strait only 56 mi (90 km) broad separates Alaska from Eurasian Siberia. This was not always so. During the last ice age, a land bridge joined the two continents. Animals and plants migrated back and forth, spreading out over both continents, for many thousands of years. This is the reason why

PACIFIC OCEAN

① Opossum
② Capuchin monkey
③ Nine banded armadillo
④ Pika
⑤ Tree porcupine
⑥ Beaver
⑦ Prairie dog
⑧ Arctic wolf
⑨ Timber wolf
⑩ Coyote
⑪ Polar bear
⑫ Kodiak bear
⑬ Grizzly bear
⑭ Black bear
⑮ Raccoon
⑯ White nosed coati

⑰ Kinkajou
⑱ Skunk
⑲ Sea otter
⑳ Wolverine
㉑ Bobcat
㉒ Puma
㉓ Northern fur seal
㉔ Californian sea lion
㉕ Elephant seal
㉖ Harp seal

㉗ Walrus
㉘ Manatee
㉙ Collared peccary
㉚ Mule deer
㉛ White-tailed deer
㉜ Elk (moose)
㉝ Caribou
㉞ Wapiti
㉟ Pronghorn antelope
㊱ American bison
㊲ Musk ox
㊳ Dall sheep
㊴ Bighorn sheep
㊵ Mountain goat
㊶ Beluga whale
㊷ Humpback whale
㊸ Gray whale

㊹ Yellow-billed loon
㊺ Anhinga
㊻ Brown pelican
㊼ Blue Heron
㊽ Blue Heron (red phase)
㊾ Wood stork
㊿ White ibis
51 Roseate spoonbill
52 Greater flamingo
53 Trumpeter swan
54 Snow goose
55 Canadian goose
56 Californian condor
57 Turkey vulture
58 Bald eagle
59 Buzzard
60 Wild turkey
61 Gambler's quail
62 Great green macaw
63 Cuban amazon
64 Roadrunner
65 Snowy owl
66 Burrowing owl
67 Elf owl
68 Quetzal
69 Rufous hummingbird
70 Anna's hummingbird
71 Sapphire-throated hummingbird
72 Toucan
73 Indigo bunting
74 Cardinal
75 Magpie

0   500   1000   1500 km

36

there are so many similarities between some North American and Eurasian species.

For example, the caribou is the American cousin of the Eurasian reindeer, and the European red deer is very much like the American Wapiti. European and Asian brown bears are related to the North American grizzly bear. There are, however, many other animal species found in the Americas that do not exist in Eurasia, including pronghorn antelope, skunk, armadillo and the tiny hummingbird.

North America remains a wide-open landscape, rich in animal life, particularly in the more thinly settled parts of Northern Canada and Alaska. The Rocky Mountains, extending from Mexico through the United States into Canada, have served as a north-south route for many different species, all the way down to the hot, dry desert. Cool, dark pine forests and rough mountain landscapes are the hunting grounds of the puma, also known as the mountain lion. The nearly extinct California condor, an enormous predatory bird with a wingspan of over 8 ft (3 m), also hunts there. The wide, grassy prairie is another typically North American environment. American bison are the habitat's largest land mammal, once travelling in enormous herds throughout the countryside. Bison were the means of survival for the Native American tribes. Smaller animals, like the prairie dog, a kind of ground squirrel, also thrive in the prairie. Many millions of these small creatures once lived in huge colonies, each inhabiting a seemingly endless network of underground chambers and tunnels. A secret tenant might be the burrowing owl, or a rattlesnake seeking shelter from the heat or cold. The coyote, a frequent character in Wild West stories or "Roadrunner" cartoons, is another resident of the prairie regions. It lives by hunting small animals, fish and carrion, but also by stealing domestic calves and lambs. For this reason, they are frequently tracked and killed by farmers. Further south, the pretty grassland gives way to dry, barren desert stretching deep into Mexico. The desert is home to the shy, but also very poisonous,

Gila monster and the speedy roadrunner. The latter survives by running down lizards and snakes. The elf owl, the world's smallest owl, lives in nest holes cut into the needled arms of the giant saguaro cactus.

The environment of most of eastern North America is wetter and greener. The entire landscape was once an enormous, endless forest before European settlers arrived to cut down the trees and put the plough to the land. A rich animal world still survives in the great lake and swamp areas. The magnificent bald eagle, with its powerful, raking talons, snatches fish out of the water in wetlands like the famous Florida Everglades. The Everglades, with its mild subtropical climate, is home to ibis, spoonbills, alligators and the

gentle manatee, also known as the sea cow.

Like a narrow bridge, Central America still joins the continents of North and South America as it has for the last 5 million years. Thousands of migratory birds make an annual journey through this land corridor, flying to and fro between their nesting places and winter quarters. The animals living in the Central American tropical rainforests are a mixture of northern and southern types. Capuchin and howler monkeys swing through the trees, while tapirs, jaguars and coatis make their way along the forest floor below. Spectacular toucans and parrots inhabit the hot lowlands. Colourful hummingbirds whirr through the air from flower to flower, their wings beating as many as 78 times per second. This allows them to virtually stand still in the air as they feed off a flower's sweet nectar.

76 Alligator snapping turtle
77 Alligator
78 Caiman
79 Rhino iguana
80 Basilisk
81 Gila monster
82 Boa
83 Rattlesnake
84 Copperhead
85 Paddlefish
86 Muskellunge
87 Pink salmon
88 Porcupine fish
89 Coral fish
90 Sea urchin

The wild mustangs of North America are descendants of European domestic breeds.

Europeans brought chaos and mindless slaughter to the great herds of bison. In 1900 there were very few remaining from the around 60 million American bison that once roamed the plains. On the very brink of extinction, a few herds were placed under protection.

This totem pole with its colourful animal carvings is evidence of the close bond of Native Americans with nature.

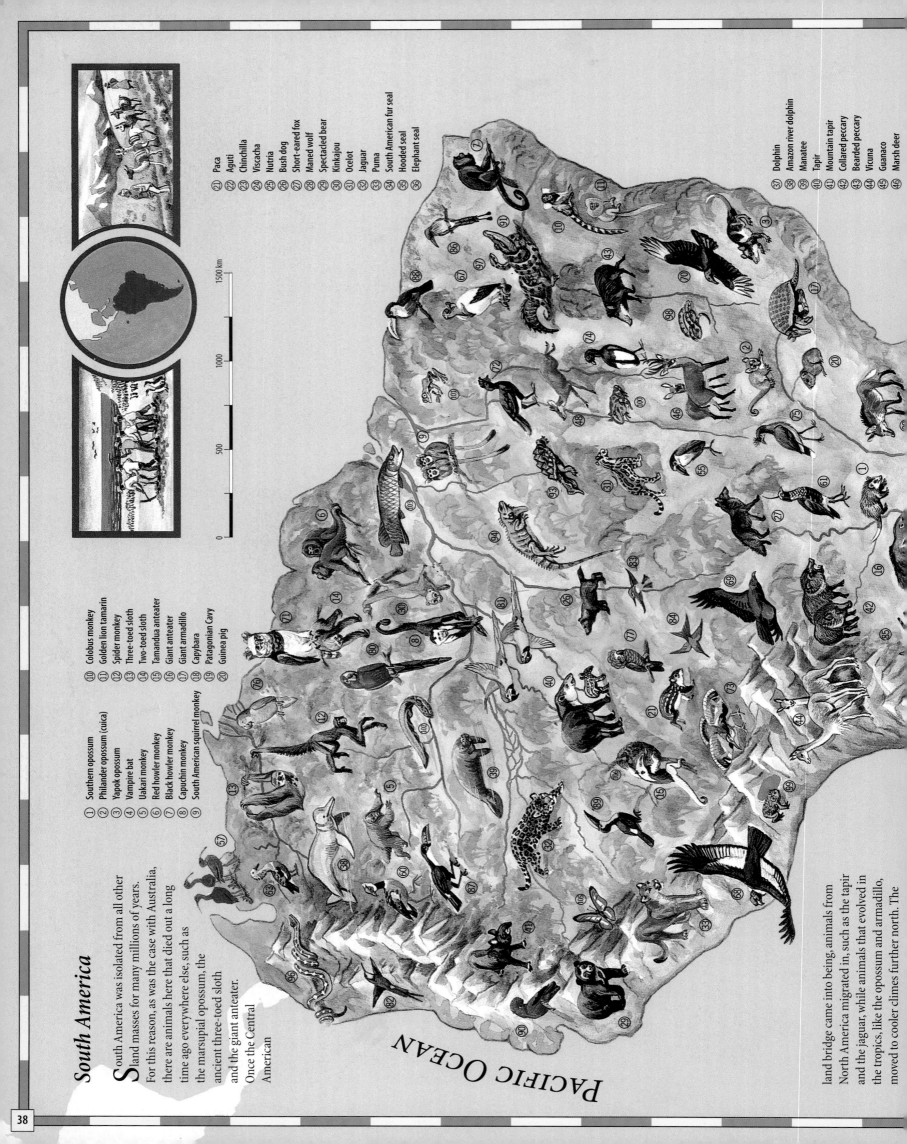

South America

South America was isolated from all other land masses for many millions of years.

For this reason, as was the case with Australia, there are animals here that died out a long time ago everywhere else, such as the marsupial opossum, the ancient three-toed sloth and the giant anteater.

Once the Central American

land bridge came into being, animals from North America migrated in, such as the tapir and the jaguar, while animals that evolved in the tropics, like the opossum and armadillo, moved to cooler climes further north. The

① Southern opossum
② Philander opossum (cuica)
③ Yapok opossum
④ Vampire bat
⑤ Uakari monkey
⑥ Red howler monkey
⑦ Black howler monkey
⑧ Capuchin monkey
⑨ South American squirrel monkey
⑩ Colobus monkey
⑪ Golden lion tamarin
⑫ Spider monkey
⑬ Three-toed sloth
⑭ Two-toed sloth
⑮ Tamandua anteater
⑯ Giant anteater
⑰ Giant armadillo
⑱ Capybara
⑲ Patagonian Cavy
⑳ Guinea pig

㉑ Paca
㉒ Aguti
㉓ Chinchilla
㉔ Viscacha
㉕ Nutria
㉖ Bush dog
㉗ Short-eared fox
㉘ Maned wolf
㉙ Spectacled bear
㉚ Kinkajou
㉛ Ocelot
㉜ Jaguar
㉝ Puma
㉞ South American fur seal
㉟ Hooded seal
㊱ Elephant seal

㊲ Dolphin
㊳ Amazon river dolphin
㊴ Manatee
㊵ Tapir
㊶ Mountain tapir
㊷ Collared peccary
㊸ Bearded peccary
㊹ Vicuna
㊺ Guanaco
㊻ Marsh deer

PACIFIC OCEAN

same is true of the guinea pig, which in South America is raised for food. The plains of the south are broad and treeless. This is the home of the maned wolf, the giant, flightless rhea and the giant anteater. The latter uses its long, thin snout and sticky tongue to extract ants and termites from their nests. Interesting animals can be found even in the extreme dryness and heat of the Atacama Desert of Chile. Every year, thousands of flamingos flock to its salty lakes searching for food. The further south one travels, the stormier the climate becomes until one reaches the southern tip of the continent, Cape Horn, and the region known as Patagonia. The icy Antarctic is not far away,

The ovenbird builds an enclosed nest out of clay and grass.

The Galapagos Islands are located in the Pacific Ocean off the north-west coast of the South American mainland. The islands are a unique animal habitat of giant land tortoises, marine iguana and the tiny Darwin finch. The islands are now a national park belonging to Ecuador.

and species like the elephant seal and South American fur seal are very much at home in the frigid coastlands. Only the green ocellated lizard survives this far south as a reminder of the tropical wonderland further north.

ATLANTIC OCEAN

(3,000 m). This often cloud-covered landscape is called the Páramo. Even here, rare species of hummingbird can be found sipping nectar. The most famous inhabitants of the Andes are the camelid species of guanacos and vicunas. These graze further south on the broad, grassy high plains. Llamas and alpacas were domesticated from wild guanaco stock by indigenous peoples many thousands of years ago. The

When threatened, the three-banded armadillo can roll itself up into an impregnable ball.

47 Andes deer (huemul)
48 Mazama deer
49 Pudu
50 Rhea
51 Humboldt penguin
52 Galapagos penguin
53 Galapagos cormorant
54 Frigate bird
55 Boat-billed heron
56 Jabiru storch
57 Scarlet ibis
58 Andes flamingo
59 Chilean flamingo
60 Crested screamer
61 Horned screamer
62 Black necked swan
63 Orinoco goose
64 Andes goose
65 Magellan goose
66 Falkland steamerduck
67 King vulture

68 Condor
69 Turkey vulture
70 Black vulture
71 Harpy eagle
72 Hokko
73 Sun bittern
74 Grey-winged trumpeter
75 Seriama
76 Amazon parrot
77 Red fan parrot
78 Slender-billed parakeet
79 Austral conure
80 Hyacinth parrot
81 Macaw
82 Topaz hummingbird
83 Little woodstar
84 Swallow-tailed hummingbird
85 Red-tailed cornet
86 Motmot
87 Giant toucan
88 Red-breasted toucan
89 Brown-backed toucan
90 Andes cock of the rock
91 Caiman
92 Galapagos giant tortoise

93 Matamata
94 Green iguana
95 Marine iguana
96 Dog-headed boa
97 Anaconda
98 Bushmaster
99 Titicaca frog
100 Horned toad
101 Monkey frog
102 Electric eel
103 Arapaima
104 Piranha
105 Blue morpho
106 Termite

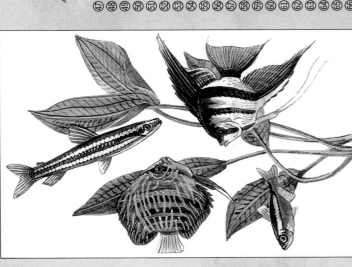

The Amazon River is home to innumerable species of colourful freshwater fish. Many Amazonian fish are popular aquarium pets.

northern half of South America is completely covered in dense rainforest, where the climate is oppressively hot and humid. The green forest canopy is inhabited not only by the hyacinth macaw, the largest parrot in the world, but also the harpy eagle, a large, predatory bird that can carry off a monkey. The fruits of the rainforest trees attract a large variety of monkeys, including the squirrel monkey, the red-furred ukari and the seldom seen golden lion tamarin. The tiny pygmy marmoset gnaws at tree bark, drinking the sap. Brightly coloured tree frogs are everywhere. Their bright red, green and yellow markings warn other animals of their poisonous skins. The famous poisoned arrows of the rain forest peoples are tipped with frog poison in preparation for the hunt. The cloudy rivers and streams of the primordial forest are home to river dolphins, anaconda snakes and piranhas.

The slopes of the Andes to the west are covered with more tranquil mountain forests at lower elevations. This is the home of the red Andean cock of the rock. The trees thin out and eventually disappear altogether at around 9,800 ft

The Arctic

Many animals living inside the Arctic Circle in the far northern regions of Europe migrate south during the bitter cold days of winter, including the snow goose and whooper swan. Those that stay behind, like lemmings and seals, must rely on a thick coat or insulating layer of blubber to keep them warm.

① Sperm whale
② Orca (killer whale)
③ Narwhale
④ Beluga
⑤ Grey whale
⑥ Blue whale
⑦ Fin whale
⑧ Sei whale
⑨ Arctic wolf
⑩ Polar bear
⑪ Walrus
⑫ Hooded seal
⑬ Bearded seal
⑭ Ribbon seal
⑮ Polar ringed seal
⑯ Harp seal
⑰ Caribou
⑱ Reindeer
⑲ Musk ox
⑳ Snow goose
㉑ Whooper swan
㉒ Greenland shark
㉓ Cod

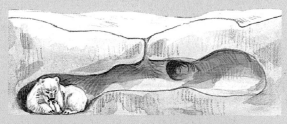

Polar bears are the largest predator of the arctic, but their cubs are born hairless, blind, deaf and barely larger than rats. Polar bears give birth in November or December in sheltered snow caves, which are warmed by body heat, just like igloos.

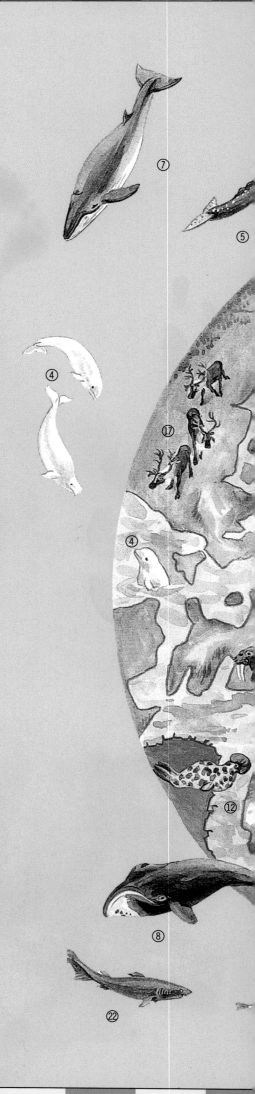

ARCTIC OCEAN

Magnetic
North Pole

North Pole

ATLANTIC OCEAN

WEDDELL SEA

South Pole

Magnetic
South Pole
+

PACIFIC OCEAN

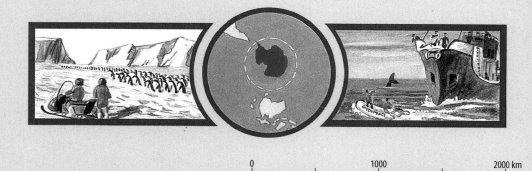

0   1000   2000 km

Antarctica

Krill, a tiny, reddish crustacean, is the most important food source in the icy south polar seas. It swarms in this part of the ocean in such great numbers that even the giant baleen whales can live off them. This is also the land of the penguins, always well dressed in their fine "tuxedos". On the ice they are waddling and inelegant, but once they dive into the sea they soar through the icy currents like arrows shot from a bow.

1. Sperm whale
2. Orca (killer whale)
3. Blue whale
4. Southern right whale
5. Humpback whale
6. Sei whale
7. Ross seal
8. Weddell seal
9. Crabeater seal
10. Leopard seal
11. Antarctic fur seal
12. Elephant seal
13. King penguin
14. Emperor penguin
15. Gentoo penguin
16. Chinstrap penguin
17. Rockhopper penguin
18. Adelie penguin
19. Cape petrel
20. Northern giant petrel
21. Southern giant petrel
22. Snow petrel
23. Antarctic cormorant
24. Snowy sheathbill
25. Skua
26. Antarctic cod
27. Mackerel icefish
28. Squid